DANNY BOY

Copyright 2025 © DS Maguar

All rights reserved. No part of this publication may be reproduced, distributed, or transmitted in any form or by any means, including photocopying, recording, or other electronic or mechanical methods, without the prior written permission of the publisher, except in the case of brief quotations embodied in critical reviews and certain other non-commercial uses permitted by copyright law.

(✱) greenhill

https://greenhillpublishing.com.au/
DS Maguar (author)
Danny Boy
ISBN 978-1-923333-80-2
SELF-HELP

Typesetting Calluna Regular 10.5/16
Cover Image by Iain Dyer
Cover and book design by Green Hill Publishing

The most important relationship you
will ever have is with yourself

DANNY BOY

DS MAGUAR

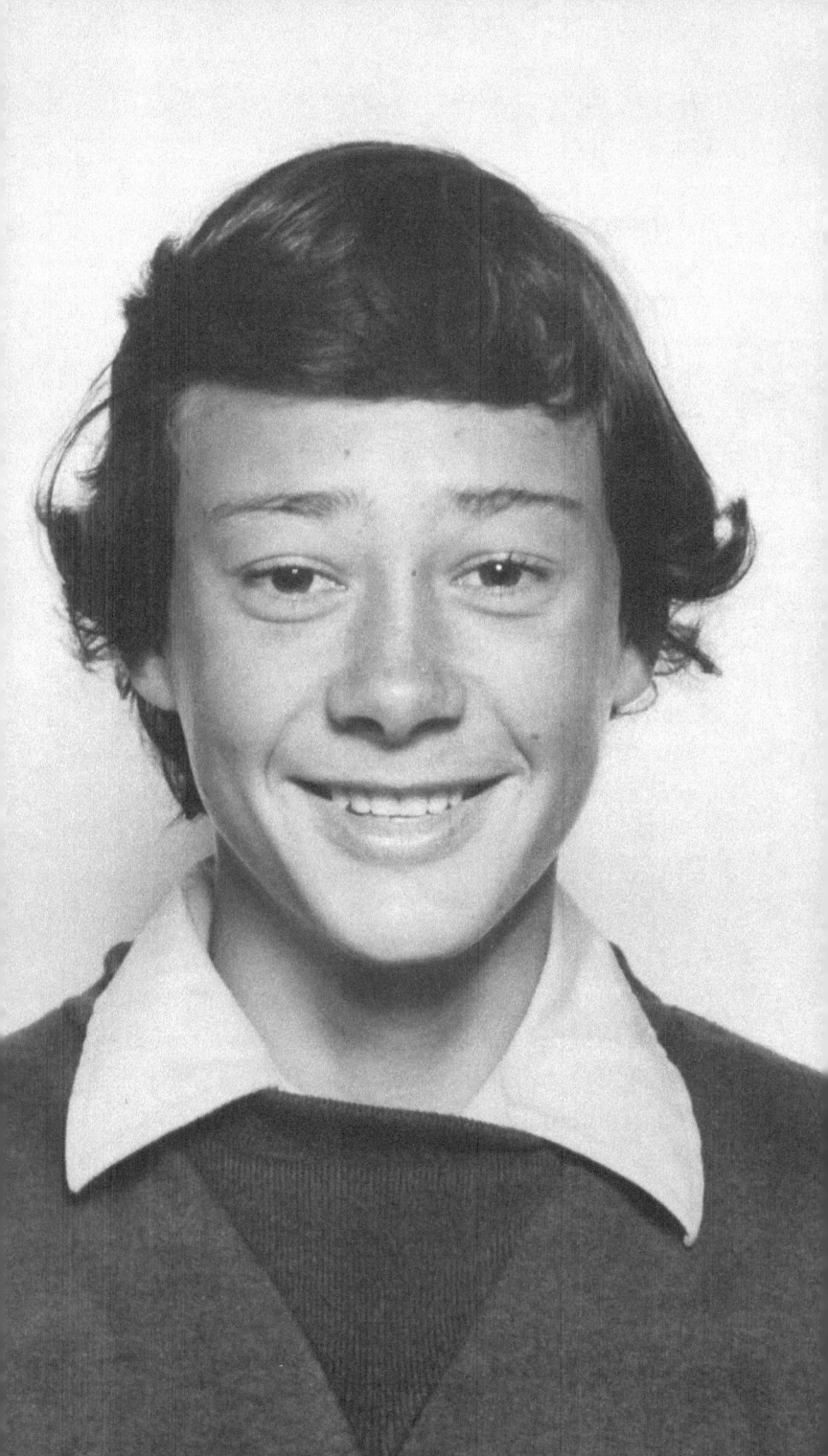

Treasure each and all the sunny days,
The twists of life, can turn, in many ways,
The clouds darken, the wind doth roar,
Towering waves crash, on an angry shore,
Life's journey will sometimes try to smother,
But to combat it all, we have each other.

Greetings, fellow travellers, along life's sometimes bumpy journey. Malcolm Fraser, then Prime Minister of Australia, observed, "Life wasn't meant to be easy."

I have known the author all my life and we have shared many of the joys and disappointments of life together. Upon completing this book, he offered me the privilege of illustrating the cover. I am not an artist, just someone who spent more time at school, drawing, than learning algebra.

The author is a man of many parts, so I had to dig deep into my psyche to ably represent the journey of the book. The journey of one man's life.

The cover. The dark cloud and lightning, rain and confused raging seas, represent the past, in particular trauma experienced as a child. The man had carried that into adult life, as represented by him, symbolically, holding hands with himself as a child. He had been through the storm many times and stood looking for a different future. This time he had managed to get through the stony grey sand and onto a patch of colour.

He realises it is decision time. Ahead lies a world of colour and promise. The blue sea and the playful dolphins, are a reminder of the joys of childhood, largely lost. The sun is in its sky, as it has been since time began. The rainbow, a divine promise, that has never been broken. He has to assimilate the traumas of the past with the joys that have come his way. He realises he must move forward, as an individual, looking at a new future. The bright unmarked sand awaits his footprints, as it turns the corner, as one must, to make change. Ahead, through the rainbow, is an endless new horizon, full of promise, new experiences and possibility. Will he take the step?

Many may see a reflection of themselves and also be encouraged to make that first step. God Bless.

Iain Dyer

*For my "A Team" with love,
thanks and gratitude*

*"Cookie cutters are best kept for Christmas.
Be uniquely different, be you."*
DS Maguar

DAN BREATHED IN THE freshness and beauty of his favourite place. He felt the sun fill him with warmth as he closed his eyes and listened to the waves breaking and the protestations of a nearby seagull.

He was home.

He marvelled at the beautiful azure colours of the crystal-clear water, for which the region was named – the Sapphire Coast, and smiled with gratitude as he remembered the journey that had brought him here just over three years ago.

Through the eyes of others, Dan had lived a highly successful life. Having left school in Grade 10 with no formal qualifications, he had worked his way up to a senior position in one of Australia's largest companies. He had status and means, but he still felt there was something missing. Dan had success but not satisfaction, and he felt no joy nor passion for life. Happiness and contentment were words he understood but didn't feel. In his mid-50s, and after two failed marriages and a failed business enterprise, Dan had reached a tipping point. Finally, the pain of not doing something different outweighed the pain of maintaining the status quo.

And so began his journey back to his true self.

Dan knew what he had become, but realised he had forgotten who he truly was. He recognised some of his limiting beliefs, habits and assumptions which he referred to as the "excess baggage" he had collected throughout his life. But he also realised that he only knew what he knew, and that there was something much deeper within him that he needed to bring to the surface and understand.

With nothing but ill ease and no firm plans, Dan packed his car and headed off on what he thought would be a short road trip. He was accompanied by his best mate and constant companion, Munay (pronounced Moonay), his four-legged three-month-old "daughter". Dan had bonded closely with Munay, a Kelpie-Border Collie-Cattle Dog cross. She had helped him navigate the void between loneliness and being alone. Munay was full of energy and playfulness, which Dan had realised was missing in him.

Born in Sydney, Dan's family had always gone north for the holidays. He had never been further south than Jervis Bay. He had never seen Candelo, a hinterland village on the far south coast of NSW where his grandmother had been born in the late 1800s. The area had recently been devastated by bushfires, so with the family connection and a desire to support the local communities, his destination was decided.

The beach had become Dan's place of peace and connection. Since they had arrived, he and Munay would go to the beach for a walk in the early morning and then again in the afternoon to play ball. It was the same daily routine, in the same location, yet magically, each day was different.

Dan would sometimes chuckle at the early memory of his grandmother, who had long passed, coming to him as he walked along the beach.

She'd said, "Get some spirit about you, lad."

Dan's grandmother was of Irish descent and not one to mess with. Her message was loud and clear and came from love.

Since that moment, Dan had felt that this was a home place, where he felt connection and belonging.

He also realised his grandmother was a part of his "A Team" (Angel Team) and was here to support him in his healing and transformation.

Today, like most days, Munay was off stalking a seagull when a young boy sitting on a log caught Dan's attention. He was drawn in by the boy's hazel eyes and the intensity and depth of his stare. His eyes were like windows to his soul. The boy sat with his arms wrapped around his knees, and without knowing how or why, Dan could feel the pain and sadness he could see in the boy's eyes.

Dan couldn't remember seeing the boy before and on an impulse, he walked up to him and said, "You look sad and in deep thought. Is everything okay?"

The boy looked up at him. "I was in deep thought until you interrupted me, but yeah, I'm okay," he replied. "I've just got some shit to deal with."

"I've not seen you here before. Are you a local?"

"Yeah, I come here every day."

"What's your name?"

"Danny."

"Well, Danny, with a name like that you must be a cool rooster. My name is Dan. Pleased to meet you. Would you like some company?"

Danny shrugged. "Sure."

"Oi, come!" Dan called, and when Munay arrived he introduced her. "This is Munay. She'll lick you to death if you let her."

"What sort of name is Munay?"

"It's a Peruvian word from the Quechuan dialect. It means unconditional love."

"That's cool, but why that name?"

"Unconditional love is a concept I'm yet to fully grasp or practise, so her name reminds me to keep working on it."

"That's weird, but it sort of makes sense."

"If you scratch her stomach, she will be your friend for life."

"She has a beautiful energy, Dan."

Dan paused for a moment. "That's a deep comment, Danny. How old are you?"

"I'm twelve. How old are you?"

"I'm fifty-eight."

"You don't look it, other than the grey hair."

"Thanks, Danny. That's kind of you to say."

"Truth is the truth, right?"

"You seem wise for your age, Danny."

"Yeah, people say I am an old soul. Do you believe in that stuff?"

"Yes, I do. It's taken me a while to make sense of it, though," said Dan.

"How so?"

"Well, Danny, part of my journey has been about remembering my true self. By true self I mean my soul self. I understand my soul self to be my intuition, the voice of disquiet that comes to me to support and guide me when I am not in balance. I grew up in a very religious family, in the Christian faith, so I get the God and Jesus thing; but all I could see was hypocrisy. It's like the true story and connection has been corrupted by interpretation and self-interest. I'm not religious, Danny, but I have a strong spiritual faith. I believe there is a universal creator from which we are all born. Every human has the creator's light within them, which is what binds us together as humanity. To me, it doesn't matter if you believe in God, Jesus, Buddha, Shiva, Mohammed or whoever else; they are all connected to the same universal source. A source of light, hope, connection and infinite strength and possibility.

"As humanity, we have lost connection to our truth. Ideological difference drives a wedge that separates us and has corrupted us because it has become all about self-interest and greed. There is enough of everything for us all to thrive in peace, yet we don't. Each of us, through our differences and unique talents and gifts, is a thread in what could be a glorious tapestry. It's an old saying, but we are one, connected by the creator's light – our soul. I think the creator's light in each of us is our soul, which is eternal. We are gifted with the opportunity to come to earth in human form to learn.

"So, Danny, getting back to your question – yes, I believe in old souls because I know I have had many past lives. There are things I know and feel that say to me, 'I have been here before.' I'm sure I have learnt plenty, but in this lifetime, I know I have plenty more to understand and learn."

"Holy crap, Dan." Danny's eyes widened. "You have a hide calling me an old soul."

"Touché, Danny, you cheeky shit. Anyway, mate, I had better keep moving. Are you sure you're okay?"

"Yeah, Dan, thanks for the chat and checking in. I might see you again?"

"I'd like that, Danny."

"Me too."

Dan continued his walk along the beach. Like most days, there weren't many people around. Dan loved solitude. The beach was his form of meditation, which began with a prayer and a conversation with his "A Team". It was a place to connect, express gratitude and, more often than not, to ask for forgiveness and answers. Dan enjoyed his daily chats with the regulars who shared his routine, but realised he knew more of the dogs' names than their owners'. He valued the comfort of their connection more than anything. Dan had often mused with those closest to him that he would be happy to live on a deserted island and interact with others by invitation only.

He didn't dislike people; he just preferred solitude. This preference was a double-edged sword. If Dan withdrew too much, he often found himself stuck in his head where he would overprocess and obsess to the point of exhaustion. As with everything in life, it was all about maintaining a healthy balance. Dan was naturally alternative and abstract in his thinking, but he also valued structure and routine. He felt safe in the order and certainty it gave him. He attributed his structure and order to what he called his "military hangover". Whilst partly true, Dan had also been reminded in a past-life reading that structure and order were the only things that had kept him alive in many past lives and were therefore deeply ingrained in him. In the past it had been about survival, literally the difference between life and death.

Dan had joined the army at the age of nineteen, and it was his life for the next eleven years. Prior to joining the army, he had been at his rebellious and undisciplined best and couldn't even see the rails, let alone fall off them. He was full of anger and resentment at everything, while smoking and drinking heavily. He had dabbled in drugs, some serious, but he had at least avoided that trap of addiction. Dan didn't lack scholastic ability, just application. His high school years had been full of unfulfilled potential. He was disruptive to the point that his principals' comment on his final Grade 10 report was, *"Dan is a clown, and I recommend on leaving school he joins a circus"*. It was also very clear that he was not welcome back.

After leaving school, Dan had found a job as a store man in an importing company. He had applied himself well, but it had all ended when the new Sales Manager, a married man with kids, had groped Dan whilst he was up a ladder. Dan had spoken to his bosses at the time, but nothing was done. The Sales Manager was more important to the business, so Dan left. He'd had a couple of other jobs since, but none of them had held any real interest.

Dan thrived in the military environment. For the first time in his adult life, he applied himself with a sense of purpose. Joining as a Private, he quickly achieved promotion to Corporal. Dan had then been encouraged to apply to The Royal Military College Duntroon to become an Officer and was successful on his second attempt. Dan studied Grade 11 and 12 as an external student to enter Duntroon. He passed with flying colours, graduated from Duntroon eighteen months later as a Lieutenant, and ultimately reached the rank of Captain. His military career ended after being medically downgraded after his second ACL reconstruction. At the loss of everything he had worked so hard for, Dan had descended back into uncertainty with anger, frustration, resentment, and depression engulfing his every thought and action. To compound the problem, he was now married and had two children under the age of two.

"Hey, Danny Boy," Dan called out when he saw Danny in the same spot the next day. "It's great to see you again. Oh sorry, is it okay to call you Danny Boy?"

"No, I don't like it, Dan. But coming from you, it seems okay."

"Did you cop all the *'Oh Danny Boy, the pipes the pipes are calling'* shit growing up?"

"Yes, I did."

"Are you sure it's okay?"

"Yeah. As I said, for some reason, I don't mind you calling me Danny Boy. So, what's been happening, Dan?"

"I've been spending a lot of time unpacking the past, mate. It's the first time I've ever taken the opportunity to really reflect on my life. I guess you could say, I'm in the midst of a personal transformation."

"Are you sure it's not a midlife crisis?"

"Yes, you cheeky shit. What do you know about midlife crisis, anyway?"

"Nothing, I just thought I would have a bit of fun with you," Danny chuckled. "What has all your unpacking taught you and why are you looking to the past for answers?"

"Good question, Danny Boy. I know I can't change the past and that the past is a moment in time I can never get back. The past only serves as a teacher and a place of learning. Hell, at one point I used to call myself a historian because I was so stuck in the past. It was only once I realised and accepted that I couldn't change it, that I started to focus more on the present. I guess I do it to look for patterns and themes to help me make sense of things.

"Spiritually, we are gifted with the opportunity to grow, and from experience, I believe that if we fail to learn, the opportunity keeps manifesting in different ways throughout our life until the lesson is learnt. It's been a bit like the onion skin analogy. When you gain new awareness from learning, it's like removing a layer of skin only to find another layer of opportunity you couldn't see before or even knew existed. At times, it's exhausting because it never seems to end, but the day we stop learning is the day we die. I'm naturally curious and like to find answers and meaning. That's why it's important to me."

"What patterns have you discovered?"

"So many questions, you're like some kind of fucking therapist, Danny Boy." Dan stopped himself. "Oh sorry, I shouldn't swear."

"Don't sweat it. I swear too. Loosen up, life's too short for regrets."

"Cheeky shit."

"I guess I'm naturally curious like you, Dan."

"You're disarming. I'm usually a very private person. I have shared more with you in our first couple of conversations than I have with most people in my lifetime."

"Is that a problem?"

"No, mate, just unusual for me. I have a habit of keeping things tucked away."

"Yeah, I sense that. How's that working for you?"

"It's kept me safe," Dan responded.

"Safe from what? The truth? At what cost?"

"Enough with the questions, Danny Boy. You're doing my fucking head in!"

"It sounds like you can do that all by yourself."

"Are you angry with me?"

"No, Danny Boy. It's just frustrating not having all the answers. That is what I meant by exhausting. Let's change the topic."

"It sounds like you're deflecting and tucking things away again, Dan."

"Enough already. What's been happening with you?"

"I've been dealing with my own shit."

"Do you want to share?" Dan asked.

"No, I will when the time is right. It's complicated... Let's just say it's hard being a good-looking young rooster from a single parent family."

"Girl troubles?"

"I wish."

"How's school?"

"Boring, I hate it. I can't see the point of half the crap they teach us. I don't understand how it's going to help me get a job."

"Sounds frustrating."

"Yeah, it is. I'm always in trouble and no one listens to me."

"I'm listening, Danny Boy."

"Thanks, Dan. I really appreciate that. I will share when it's the right time. And when you are ready."

"What do you mean by that?"

"You'll understand in time..."

"I don't believe in coincidence, Danny Boy. Everything happens for a reason. I feel as if we know each other, even though we've only just met."

"I feel the same," Danny said.

"I'm glad we met, Danny Boy."

"Me too."

"We definitely have one thing in common: a dislike of school. It wasn't until I was nineteen that I completed Grade 12. I was in the Army at the time and needed it to get into officer training. Without that, I doubt I would ever have done it. I aced it at the time and got the highest score in the state for English, which was rather fortunate. I remember my teacher asking me how the final exam had gone. I told him I had really struggled with the self-reading question which constituted 30% of the exam. Everything I had read didn't fit the question. He was concerned, but I told him not to worry and that it would be okay because I had made up a story on the spot called *Only A Boy* which was easy to quote from. My teacher was horrified by what I had done."

"What if the examiners ask for a copy of the book you referenced?" his teacher had asked.

"I'll have to write it quickly, won't I?"

"You put everything you worked so hard for at risk. If they disqualify you, there will be no Duntroon.

Who's the cheeky shit now, Dan? What made you do it?"

"I thought it showed initiative and adaptability. After an uncomfortable two month wait for the results, all I could do was laugh when I got a Very High Achievement and top score in the state. I wouldn't do it again or recommend that anyone else ever does it. I got away with it, but being in the army at the time... let's just say I dodged a bullet. No one was more relieved than my teacher. I appreciated his concern had come from a place of genuine care and I was glad that things worked out okay in the end. He was the only schoolteacher in my life that I rated and really appreciated."

"What was it like being in the army?"

"Mate, I really enjoyed it. I loved the mateship and camaraderie. It gave me a sense of belonging. It was a different world, but one I enjoyed."

"How did you go with the discipline and structure?"

"I accepted it, but I often attracted attention for the wrong reason. Calling me head strong is an understatement. I never enjoyed basic training, but in a sense, it toughened me up. I was able to find a way through it. When I went to my first posting, it was like a normal job, just in uniform. The gap between ending basic training and going to my first unit was eventful though. At the end of basic training at Kapooka, I was allocated to the Royal Australian Corps of Transport as a Movement Control Officer."

"What's that?"

"It's a bit like the army's travel agency. The next course to get my qualifications wasn't for another six months, so I was sent to Puckapunyal to do general duties until my course started. That basically meant marking time doing menial shit like washing dixies – pots and pans – in the mess. It was as boring as hell. I started to become outspoken and resentful and the Warrant Officer in charge of me started to ride me hard. I was always getting extra duties and allocated the shittier jobs. I've learnt being bored, frustrated and resentful is not a good place for me. It surfaced negativity and anger in me which only led to more trouble. I was on a downward spiral and blaming everyone and everything for what was being done to me. It took me many years and frustrations to realise I was creating my own nightmare. I have since coined a phrase I now live by: **"Externalise for satisfaction, internalise for opportunity."**

"What does that mean?" Danny asked.

"Basically, mate, it means you have to find an outlet to release your anger and frustration, then look for opportunity within your control to achieve a better outcome. When you externalise blame to others, nothing changes other than your frustration levels. It's not our job to change others; the only person you can change is yourself. What I'm saying is, you have to let go of the anger and frustration you think others have caused you, then ask yourself, *'what did I do to cause or contribute to the situation?'* And *'what can I do to change the result?'* In this case, rather than blaming everyone else for what was happening, I could have owned it and realised I was causing the outcome I didn't like and change my behaviour. That's another thing I have learnt: **"change your association to change the outcome."**

"And what does that mean?"

"We all have the power to change any negative situation into a positive. It's a choice only we can make. Anger and frustration leave us powerless, but when we internalise it, we create infinite possibility which gives us the power to make positive changes as opposed to being the victim of what's being done to us."

"How do you release frustration?"

"These days, mate, I yell at trees. It's good for me but probably not the tree. Frustration is a normal emotion we all experience. I used to exercise to run it out, but now I find it more effective to just release it from my body. Everyone is different. It doesn't matter if you yell, run, punch a bag or hit hard on the footy field, the most important thing is to let the frustration go. It's only then that you can be calm and rational and truly get into a state where you can see your opportunity.

"With this simple understanding, I could have prevented so many negative situations in my life. Life is a journey of learning. At times, I'm a slow learner. I can't change the past, but this simple learning and practice now gives me the opportunity to change and positively influence today and the future. I'm so grateful that I finally learnt this lesson. Those six months could have been so different with the wisdom of hindsight. They were unnecessarily tough based on the choices I made at the time. That period was also defined by two memories. One funny, the other traumatic."

"What happened?" Danny asked, listening intently.

"I was working at the Mess Hall and all the staff had been complaining about an emu that kept getting into the garbage and crapping everywhere. They had tried to shoo it away without success and the problem had been ongoing for over two weeks. I had seen the emu hanging around, so I decided to see if I could solve the problem. I grabbed some stale bread and laced it with some tabasco sauce and went to the rear of the mess, where the emu readily approached me for a free feed. The emu gulped the bread down and stood still, looking for more until the tabasco kicked in. Its eyes suddenly bulged open and it took off running in circles, making a loud hooting noise. It ran around for about two minutes until it finally did the splits and sat on the ground just hooting. I swear I could see steam coming out of its ears. Mate, it was the funniest thing I have ever seen, and I can't remember laughing so hard in my life. It was one hell of a sight. After about five minutes, the emu took off, never to be seen again. I love animals and so it suddenly dawned on me that what I did, albeit effective, was actually cruel. I had solved the problem but after the incident was reported, the only thanks I got was a stern talking to and another two weeks of extra duties."

"You certainly had a mischievous streak, Dan. Surely you knew there would be consequences?"

"Back then, I had a habit of not thinking things through. On another occasion, I thought I would send my commanding officer a ransom note for his prized gold fish. Let's just say taking a photocopy of a fish never ends well, but that's another story. The second memory was karmic debt and nowhere near as funny."

Danny's eyes widened. "What happened?"

"I was invited to a friend of a friend's brother's twenty-first birthday party. It was in a town in country Victoria, so it was a chance to get off base, get away from my mundane routine, and have some fun. The other two people, a couple who I met on the night, were in the army too and had completed their basic training and were posted there. I had offered to be the designated driver and had no plans for a big night. The party was okay, and I was enjoying myself until bizarrely, during the speeches, the parents announced they were separating. To that point, none of our group had hit the grog that hard, but that all changed after the speeches. On hearing her parents' news, the girl hit the bottle and ended up off her face.

"We left the party around 1:30am, and as agreed, I was driving. All began smoothly until the girl started saying it was her car and she wanted to drive. I tried to calm her down, but she was off her face. She was sitting behind me in the rear passenger seat when she reached forward and put her arms around my neck, insisting that she wanted to drive. I slowed down and pulled the car over to the side of the road, all the while trying to release her suffocating grip around my neck. She lunged at me again, kicking, punching, and screaming, trying to get the keys out of my hand. Without thinking, I threw the keys into the long grass in the paddock we had pulled up next to and suggested none of us were going anywhere. It stopped her aggression and argument, but with her on hands and knees in near total darkness, she managed to locate the keys! I had two choices."

"What were they?"

"I could either stay in the middle of nowhere with no idea where I was or how to get back to base, or I could take my chances and get back into the car. I knew I would be charged with being AWOL – absent without leave – if I didn't get back to base, so I got back into the car. It was a decision that nearly cost me my life. Initially, her driving wasn't that bad, but that all changed as the grog continued to kick in and she started to become fatigued. She progressively drove more and more erratically. We reached speeds above 160km, and she was swerving all over the road. I was now in the rear left passenger seat, and nothing can describe the absolute fear I felt. I felt physically ill. All requests to slow down fell on deaf ears. All I could do was sit there and wait for us to crash. I prayed, asked for forgiveness, stated my last rights, and said goodbye to my family. I knew it wasn't going to end well. Saying goodbye gave me a sense of peace and I relaxed slightly."

"What happened next?"

"The car hit the wall in a cut-through at about 140km per hour and rolled end over end multiple times. I remember the first impact and roll, but I blacked out after that. When the car finally came to rest, I realised I was banged up but still alive. I checked my mate beside me who was conscious, but he had blood all over him and was missing some fingers on his left hand. I then checked the girl's boyfriend, who was in the front passenger seat. He was amazingly unhurt, but the girl was not in the car. She wasn't wearing a seatbelt so had been thrown out of the car. I applied basic first aid to my mate and then the adrenalin kicked in. I realised we were still vulnerable, and my only thought was to get out of the car, alert other drivers, find the girl, and get help.

"The car was a crumpled mess, and my only way out was through what was left of the back windscreen. I crawled out and tried to warn and flag down oncoming vehicles. I nearly got run over twice in the attempt before I was finally able to get some help from some passing motorists who pulled over and helped. They sat me down, set up a warning for oncoming traffic and called 000. I gave them an appraisal of the two in the car and said the driver was missing. When they arrived, they located her, and somehow, she was still alive.

"It wasn't until I got back to the base hospital that shock set in. I knew I was covered in blood but had no idea of the extent of the damage. I lost all control of my body and began to shake violently when they placed me on a table to assess my injuries. The adrenalin had allowed me to function until that point, but I remember literally bouncing off the table after that. They sedated me and all I remember was lying there for what seemed like hours. My chin had been sliced open and the skin flap was lodged in my ear, and I had multiple deep lacerations all over my face and head. My nose had been sliced above my lips and the skin was at right angles to my exposed nose bones. I was a right royal mess but didn't find out about my injuries until I looked in the mirror in the following day.

"It was about 5:30am when they transferred me into bed. I immediately fell into a deep exhausted sleep. In true military fashion, I was woken up at 6:00am to be given a sleeping tablet. It had been an incredibly traumatic experience to that point, but nothing prepared me for the trauma of seeing myself for the first time. I was woken up mid-morning to have a shower. I was in a lot of pain, but they explained that I needed to wash the dried blood away to help support the healing of my injuries. I screamed when I saw my reflection in the mirror. I looked like the elephant man. My head was swollen to more than twice its normal size and I had hundreds of stitches all over my head and face. I almost passed out. They tried to calm me, but all I could do was stare at the abomination in the mirror and cry.

"They notified my family of the accident and the next day my mother came to see me after driving overnight. I remember seeing her enter the ward. It was about fifty meters long with beds on either side. I watched her slowly make her way past the first couple beds, looking out for me as she went. When she approached my bed, she gave me a sympathetic smile and kept walking. She couldn't recognise her own son! I called out to her; she glanced back and her face froze in realisation. It was incredibly hard for her because my stepsister had been in a car accident a few years earlier that had left her in a coma for over six weeks and with permanent brain stem damage. Again, in true military style, the only message my mother got from the Duty

Officer was that I had been in an accident but I wasn't dead. My mother tried to cover her shock, but her eyes betrayed her bravado.

"We were all incredibly lucky to survive that night. I received over 150 stitches to my head and face. When the car rolled, even though I had my seatbelt on, my head had gone through the rear windscreen which is what had caused my injuries. I was in hospital for three weeks before I was released on convalescence leave. The physical healing took time, but the emotional healing took a lot longer. Like most nineteen-year-olds, I thought I was ten foot tall and bullet proof. The accident changed that. I thought I was going to be physically scarred for the rest of my life. In my mind, I had gone from being a fit, strong, confident good looking young rooster to an ugly, fearful, self-conscious 'thing'."

"It sounds like it was a tough time, Dan," Danny responded.

"It was, Danny Boy. After recounting it to you, I'm not sure I'm completely over it, even now. It's stirred up some deep emotions. Physically looking at me today, you can barely see the scars. Emotionally, I am still carrying some of the trauma. But thank you, Danny Boy. It's helped me to talk about it after all these years."

"I didn't do anything."

"Yes, you did. You listened. Listening to someone, without comment or judgement, is one of the greatest gifts you can give them. In sharing that experience with you, it's given me the opportunity to see that I'm not *fine*, and that I still have more healing to do so I can fully release the impacts of that trauma."

"My pleasure, Dan. I'm happy to help... I think?"

***

"HEY, DAN!" DANNY WAVED Dan over. "I haven't seen you for a couple of weeks."

"Gidday, Danny Boy, it's great to see you again. I've been away working up in Central Queensland."

"What do you do for work?"

"I'm a leadership and personal development coach and mentor."

"Cool, what led you to that?"

"A deep sense of purpose, I guess. I love giving of myself in support of others. For much of my life, I was focused on what I could get out of life and not what I could give. Joy isn't an emotion I often experience, but I feel joyful in giving of myself. We all have a story, mate. My story has been colourful, and I have experienced plenty of positive and negative learnings throughout my life. In sharing my learnings with others, my goal is to help unlock potential and create possibility. I see giving of myself as my gift to humanity, and there is no greater feeling of satisfaction than supporting others to grow."

"It sounds like you actually care, Dan."

"I do care," Dan said thoughtfully. "Caring and giving of myself gives me energy. The opportunity to give of myself is the greatest gift I have been given in my life. When I do it, I feel connected, in balance and in flow. For me, it's like a feel-good drug. If we all gave more freely of ourselves, we would live in a much better world. Understanding the feeling of flow has also helped me effectively recognise when I'm out of balance or flow.

"After we last spoke and before I went away, I had an overwhelming feeling of anxiety. I felt physically tight in my chest and very vulnerable, fearful and unsafe. The anxiety was related to reliving the accident I spoke about. They say time heals, which is true, but whilst we might find a way to move forward at the time, if we carry unresolved emotional association, all we do is create emotional excess baggage. All I can say is, I'm glad I haven't had to pay for the excess baggage I have carried. It would have cost me more than my life's earnings. That said, I have paid a huge price in other ways. Thanks, Danny Boy, for helping me to see some of the baggage I was carrying that I still needed to release."

"How did you release it?"

"Firstly, I recognised what I was feeling. The anxiety I felt clearly indicated that I hadn't fully released the emotional impacts of that experience. I then started to breathe in and out deeply and went through a process in my head of bundling all the negative emotions into a box, putting a ribbon on it and giving the gift of understanding back to the universe by taking a big breath in and blowing the negativity away."

"Does that shit actually work?"

"Yes, mate, the constriction in my chest disappeared

along with the feeling of anxiety. I have more to unpack, but I guess it's an example of how we can change our state in the moment. Trying to problem solve in a state of anxiety doesn't work. It's only when we are calm that we can ask the right questions to unpack the situation."

"What do you mean by asking the right question?"

"You just answered your own question, Danny Boy."

"How?"

"You asked 'what', not 'why'. I call it '**the power of what**'. Mate, I practice natural health, eat organic food and I'm pharmacy drug free, yet I smoke a pipe; and before you ask, only tobacco. Asking why I smoke, given I know it's bad for my health and could kill me, is near impossible to answer. In asking myself that question, I can't give you a single logical reason or answer as to why I do it. I can give you heaps of reasons why I shouldn't smoke, yet it doesn't stop me. They say change can only occur when the pain or consequence of not doing something is greater than the pain or consequence of what you are currently doing. Currently, I have no motivator for change regardless of the known risks. I simply can't tell you why I smoke. That's where the 'power of what' kicks in. What is the source of my addiction? What do I use smoking to mask? What could I change to become a non-smoker? What created my need to smoke? These are questions that can be explored for understanding and can be answered. Sure, it will take effort and focus, but you can answer 'what' questions. I spent so much energy asking why I caused myself to have a partial mental breakdown. Asking 'why' is often unanswerable but asking 'what' creates possibility and will more likely lead to an answer."

"So, *what* are you doing about not smoking, Dan?"

"I have a goal to be addiction free by the end of the year."

"I'll hold you to that."

"Don't worry, mate. Most importantly, I will hold myself to that," Dan said.

"So, by sharing your stories with me, does that make you my coach?"

"Yes, in a sense, I guess it does. But based on the number of questions you ask, I'm not sure who is coaching who."

"Good question, Dan. Who is coaching the coach?"

"You're relentless, Danny Boy." Dan shook his head.

"It's fun and I'm enjoying it. Besides, it sounds like you could do with help."

"Cheeky shit! You're an enigma, Danny Boy. One of my natural gifts is the ability to understand and read people. At times you leave me perplexed. You're twelve years old with the wisdom of a ninety-year-old and have a deep sense of knowing. I can't get a fix on you."

"You'll get a fix on me soon enough, Dan. Like you, just know I care."

***

DAN WAS ANGRY AND bitter about how his time in the army had ended. He was now married with two children under the age of two. He had no job to go to and his only plan was to relocate the family from Townsville to Tasmania and start again. Things were tough for the first three years. Dan was externalising blame to everyone but himself and subsequently referred to that time as "the wasted years". He finally realised he and his attitude were the cause for everything being against him and not working out. Once he internalised the opportunity, things started to change for the better. Like when he left school, Dan had several jobs that didn't motivate or excite him, but they were essential to providing for his family. He was always very serious, often angry and rarely at peace.

After ten years, his marriage ended. Whatever Dan did, it was never enough in his wife's eyes. The harder he tried and the more he gave, the more that was demanded and expected of him. He felt he couldn't win or ever make his wife happy. His frustrations and resentment toward her built and externally manifested when he lashed out and slapped his son across the face. Dan's anger was with his wife, not his son, but he didn't know how to deal with it. He had tried everything he could to make things work, but at the time, he wasn't equipped to find a solution. His wife had said, "I am setting you free", but Dan would carry the regret of what he had done to his son far more than the loss of his marriage.

True to her word, Dan's wife would make him pay for taking the best years of her life. His wife used the children as pawns for payback. Dan thought it had been tough dealing with his remorse over what he had done to his son, but nothing compared to the devastation he felt sitting alone beside an empty Christmas Tree on the first Christmas morning after he and his wife had separated. Dan had never experienced grief like it. He sat there and cried and cried until he could cry no more. He had lost his children. Dan judged himself as a failure of a father: he had always been so busy trying to make things right that he rarely fully enjoyed just being dad with his kids. It wasn't until they were gone that he felt such a deep sense of loss. Dan's kids were ten and eight when his marriage ended, and he subsequently played a limited role in their upbringing from that point on. In his wife's words: "there is only one family, and you are no longer a part of it". Dan's "freedom" certainly came at a huge cost.

***

A FATHER'S PROMISE – For My Kids

I heard no harps playing or angels singing when you entered my world.

I wasn't ready to receive you as the gift you have become.

Through the years of separation and heartbreak we shared our pain in isolation.

If not for the love and encouragement from the sweetest angel, I would have given up.

Hope, tears, more hope, and more tears was all I had.

Anger, hurt and frustration were my excuses for what I did and didn't do.

I was born perfectly imperfect, but did the best I could do with what I had and who I was at the time.

I caused you hurt and pain, which I recognise, own and lament, but cannot change.

My darkest days and deepest grief came with the realisation you were gone from my life.

I came to understand the connection and love I had for you was greater than anything else.

You are a part of me today and forever more.

Dream of the impossible until it becomes possible, and...

Know with absolute certainty that now and when I am gone,
I will guide you, encourage you, support you, but above all else, I will love you.
The love for a partner can come and go.
But a father's love for his child is forever.
Thank you for the gift you are to me my beautiful children.

❉❉❉

"FANCY SEEING YOU HERE, Danny Boy!"

"Gidday, Dan. What's been happening?"

"It's always about me," Dan said, taking a seat next to Danny. "I'd like to learn more about you. When we first met, you mentioned you were dealing with your own shit. Do you want to share?"

"Yeah, I'm trying to understand why my best mate doesn't want me around anymore."

"Is that what he said?"

"No, but that's what it feels like. We used to hang out together all the time. We would look up into the sky and watch the clouds, daydreaming and sharing our hopes and dreams for the future. We were always laughing and having fun talking shit. Then one day he just cut me out. It was like I didn't exist. I know I didn't do anything wrong, but something changed in him."

"Do you know what it could have been?"

"Yeah, I think I know, but I don't think he knows. I tried to talk to him about it, but he just shut me out. It really sucks. I let him know that I would always be his mate and there for him, which for now, is all I can do. In time, I hope we become best mates again, but for now I just have to wait and be there for him when he needs me."

"How likely do you think that is?" Dan asked.

"It'll happen when he's ready and when the time is right."

"You sound certain."

"I am."

"So, what's been happening in your world, Coach?"

"I successfully became a non-smoker, you cheeky shit."

"Well done, Dan. What changed?"

"I have always recognised that my **health is my true wealth.** In the end, I made the choice to love and value myself and put my health first again. I tied the change to a mantra I created for myself – 'I will thy will for Dan, for he is worthy'. I would say it whenever I felt like smoking until I no longer did. It gave me the strength and resolve I needed to make the change."

"You just quit cold turkey?"

"Yes, mate. Anything is possible if you frame it positively," Dan said.

"Say that again?"

"Saying 'I can't' is a self-fulfilling prophecy, whereas saying 'I can, when or if' creates infinite possibility and a positive solution in your mind. I plan to take the same approach to changing another lifelong pattern I've gained awareness around."

"What's that?"

"I am highly self-critical and self-sabotaging when I judge myself as having failed. Rather than being addicted to alcohol, I have used it as a crutch and my torturer.

By drinking, I have created a habit of escaping from my own perceived failings. Alcohol has also been the source of many poor decisions which have compounded negativity and self-judgement. Getting drunk was an escape, not a solution. Rather than escape, I need to understand and deal with my issues, instead of tucking them away and having them fester, unresolved."

"Do you plan to become a non-drinker?"

"Yes, mate. I think that's what it will take to truly change the pattern. I have tried in the past without success, but I know it's something I need to own and master in order to be truly happy. For now, I am starting with 'Dry July', but I know I must dig deeper than just abstinence to change the habit. There is a lot to unpack, but I am ready. It all starts with being aware of the problem and owning it. **Awareness creates opportunity for change, not justification and excuse for not changing.** I've spent too much time on the excuse side."

"Why's that?"

"Fear, mate!"

"Of what?"

"Judgement, failure, not belonging, being different, you name it. Fear is a strong motivator. I created a model I use in coaching that best illustrates what I mean."

"What's the model?"

"It's called 'The Fear Model'."

THE FEAR MODEL

EXCUSE	OPPORTUNITY
Fuck	Focus
Everything	Efforts to
And	Achieve different
Run	Results

"We are all born with an inherent fight or flight mechanism. Originally, it was to keep us safe in a hostile and dangerous environment. Over time the adversity and consequences have diminished and now our flight mechanism is more often triggered to avoid unpleasant situations as opposed to dangerous ones. It has become more of a passive-aggressive avoidance strategy. The tendency on the excuse side of fear is to not deal with or confront our fears. In doing so, we limit our growth and opportunity to learn, and only serve to increase our frustrations around things seemingly not changing. The frustration can also manifest into anger. **Not facing one's fear is a self-imposed limitation. Personal freedom is not taken away, it's given away.** We always have a choice. If we choose to face our fears by testing our limiting beliefs and assumptions, we create opportunities for new learning and positive change. As I have already said, we all have a choice to change any outcome or fear by changing our association to it. We have the control to be free.

"When I was in the army, they taught me that if ambushed, the best defence was attack. Rather than stand still and be shot, we were taught to turn and face the enemy and charge, all guns blazing whilst screaming like a banshee. Either way, the likelihood of survival was low, but the thinking was that it was better to do something that gave you some chance than stay still and await certain death. If our self-talk is the enemy, the same principle applies. We can allow our thoughts to become our reality and wait for something to happen to us that we don't want, or we can change our self-talk and change the outcome. It all starts with recognising what we are fearful of. **Know fear to have no fear.** If we understand our limiting belief or negative self-talk (our fear), we can test it, own it, confront it and defeat it. It may feel that things happen to us, but in truth they happen for us. We can choose to think it has been done to us and respond like a victim or choose to think it has been done for us and choose to learn and grow. We can choose to be a victim, but in truth, **we are only ever the victim of our own choices,** which is something within our control to change."

"You must spend a lot of time in your head. What do you do to relax and have fun and just enjoy being in the moment?" Danny asked.

"Fancy you asking another probing question, Danny Boy. Where do you get them from?"

"Curiosity and the need to understand. By the way, you still haven't answered me. Is that passive avoidance?"

"No, you cheeky shit. I love to connect to nature. Whether that's watching leaves covered in dew, sparkling in the morning sunlight, or sitting on the grass under my favourite Jacaranda tree looking for pictures in the sky, or walking on the beach watching the seals and dolphins at play. For me, they are all forms of meditation, gifted to me by the beauty of creation. I have always struggled to find peace. I've tried yoga and different forms of meditation and breathwork, but it's only when I'm in nature that I can press pause on my hyperactive brainbox and connect.

"By definition, we are called human beings, but like most people, I spend more than 97% of the time as 'human' and less than 3% just 'being' in the moment. It takes conscious effort to put yourself in the moment. I guess that's why I love the beach so much. The beach is like my place of meditation. It's also a wonderful metaphor for life. I'm often the first to leave a footprint in the sand. In that moment, the path is clear in front of me (opportunity), and as the waves break, the wash removes the footprints of where I have been (the past), and that just leaves me in the present. Every new moment in time is uniquely different and full of unlimited possibilities. In the moment, the past or future doesn't exist. We can't change the past or predict the future, but we can make unlimited changes in the present. It's only our thoughts and habits that limit opportunity, not the moment itself. We are the producer, director and lead actor in our life. We have the power to change the script at any time if we choose to. **Our reality is self-imposed. If we don't like our reality, we have the power to change it."**

"Is that how you plan to unpack your association with alcohol?"

"Yes, mate, it is."

"How will that work?"

"In my job prior to coaching, I was in business improvement. A big part of the role was problem solving. Over time, I learnt the best way to problem solve was to **think solution, not problem.** One of the key business improvement tools I was taught was the '5 Whys'. The principle behind the tool was to be like a child and to keep asking 'why' until you have a solution. It sounded easy, but I always found it hard to apply. Often, you end up going down a rabbit hole and come up with a root cause that if rectified wouldn't stop the problem from happening again. By focusing on the problem, we naturally associate it with a negative bias because something has gone wrong. When we think about a solution, we look at the problem from a positive opportunity perspective, which forces us to think outside the box and engage in creative thinking.

"It also ties back directly to the power of asking 'what', not 'why'. How we approach unpacking our limiting beliefs, assumptions and habits is critical to the results we get. If we approach the problem by asking 'why' or from a negative association, we will likely find excuses and justifications, not solutions. If our self-talk is 'I can't, because...' psychologically, the result becomes a self-fulfilling prophecy. Alternatively, if we change our self-talk to 'I can, if, or when...' we create possibility and a positive opportunity to find solutions that will more likely result in positive and sustainable change. I guess that's what I mean when I say change the association to change the outcome."

"What caused you to use alcohol as a crutch?" Danny asked.

"That one is a bit like an octopus with multiple tentacles, Danny Boy. I started drinking at a very early age, probably not much older than you are now. From there it's just always been a part of my life."

"What caused you to drink at such a young age?"

"I'm not sure. I haven't fully unpacked it yet. Like I said, it's a bit like an octopus. There are cultural, behavioural and environmental contributing factors. Like most young males in Australia, I initially drank to have fun and be sociable. Culturally, it was part of a rite of passage into adulthood, then over time it became behavioural as I used it as an escape."

"What were you escaping from?"

"Throughout my life I have experienced my fair share of trauma and heartbreak. Rather than find a way to release it, I created a pattern of just locking it away inside and moving on. It was my coping mechanism, but all it served was the need to escape from the pain of my unresolved emotions. This coping mechanism has significantly affected my closest relationships as well. I became dependent on others to resolve situations I felt uncomfortable in, rather than speaking my truth and dealing with things directly myself. I had the mental strength to move on, but I carried a huge amount of unresolved emotional baggage with me. For much of my life, it has been like sailing in a boat with a huge tail wind but with the anchor down. I've made progress, but it's been tough going on me as well as those closest to me."

"And what's been the anchor?"

"I've always been extremely self-critical and quick to focus on my shortcomings and mistakes. I've lived my life with a deficit focus and have never forgiven myself for being human. I'm not naturally a perfectionist, but when it comes to personal standards I set for myself, I am. I know that by design I am perfectly imperfect and will make mistakes, but up until recently, I have been a highly effective self-judge and executioner. At times, this has led to intense low personal worth and self-esteem. Drinking alcohol became an escape from the unresolved emotional issues which then descended into a habit of self-punishment for all my 'failures'."

"So, what's changed?"

"Well, for starters, being more aware and accepting of what I feel. It sounds simple but, **you can't think your way to how you feel.** I have always been mentally strong, but emotionally weak. I have a high level of EQ (Emotional Intelligence) when dealing with others, but not myself. I have an engrained care for others but until recently I didn't extend the same love and care to myself. I have used alcohol to punish myself for being imperfect."

"So, what led to becoming more emotionally aware?"

"Asking 'what', not 'why'. And Pachamama—"

"—Pacha what?"

"Pachamama. It's the Peruvian word for 'The Mother': like Mother Nature, Mother Earth. In Peru, they have a ceremony that incorporates ayahuasca, to help connect to Pachamama and higher spiritual realms. Native Peruvian Shamans utilise ayahuasca as a natural medicine to treat physical and emotional illness. The shaman can go on your journey with you and gain insight as to the cause of your problems. For me, it was all emotional and spiritual sickness."

"What's ayahuasca and how does it work?"

"Ayahuasca is a drink produced by boiling the roots and leaves of two different plants found in The Amazon rainforests. The roots represent both the masculine and feminine and neither have any effect in isolation from the other. Ayahuasca gets a mixed wrap because of its narcotic and hallucinogenic properties. Some people think it's just a drug hit, like taking acid in the 60s, but that's not how I experienced it. For me, the ceremonies and rituals associated with it and its effects on me were a life-changing medicinal tonic. There are reported ongoing negative impacts from taking ayahuasca, which I didn't experience. For me, it was the most confronting but positively impactful experience of my life."

"What led you to taking it?"

"I love to travel, Danny Boy, and I have been fortunate to see and experience many other countries and cultures. I first became aware of ayahuasca when I visited Peru to do the Inca Trail trek. As part of the trip, I saw what looked like dead sticks for sale in a market in Cusco. When I asked about them, I was introduced to the story of Ayahuasca medicine. Visiting Peru and doing the Inca Trail was such a wonderful, spiritually uplifting experience for me. I fell in love with Peru and its people, who were all joyous and happy. By our standards they had nothing, yet their joy, smiles and warmth made them the richest and happiest people I had ever encountered. Their energy matched the beauty of the Andes and their environment. Whilst not realising it at the time, experiencing Peru was the start of my personal spiritual awakening and transformation."

"Did you do Ayahuasca as part of that trip?"

"No, mate, I did it a couple of years after. Ayahuasca was a spiritual calling. People who want it or treat it as a drug high inevitably come away disappointed. It's much more than a high, or a vivid hallucination or psychedelic vision. For me, it was the medicine of connection, and I was called to do it by Pachamama."

Danny tilted his head. "What do you mean by being 'called'?"

"After visiting Peru, I started to question what I was doing in life. Although I had a great job, had remarried, had a wonderful wife and I was in great health, I still found that I had no joy, fulfillment nor a feeling of satisfaction in my life. For all intents and purposes, I was the perfect slave to what I had been told success was and what it looked like. I had seen unbridled joy and happiness in the Peruvian people and had started to question what was missing in me. One day whilst I was cycling, a clear thought came into my head. It was that I needed to go to Peru and participate in Ayahuasca. That's what I mean when I say it's a spiritual calling. The message was like a lightning bolt that struck. It came out of the blue, but clearly.

"I remember riding home and telling my wife about the

message and the decision I had made to go back to Peru. She had tears in her eyes, she was so excited for me. And more than anyone, including myself, she understood why it was important for me to do it. My wife had witnessed first-hand the unhappiness that was locked deep within me. Earlier in our marriage, she had challenged me around my interests and hobbies outside of work and had asked me what made me joyous and happy. A particular question she asked me was, 'are you dying to live or living to die?' The answer saddened me because I realised I was living to die. My wife had also seen me escape into my alcoholic stupors, and as much as we loved each other, she could only be saddened by what she saw me doing to myself. In the end, it was what led to my decision to end our marriage some years later. I loved her too much to keep hurting her and sadly, I knew at the time I couldn't trust myself not to 'escape' again."

"So, what happened in Peru?"

"Mate, it's getting dark. I had better get moving. Munay is champing at the bit to get some exercise and have a bit of a play."

"That's not fair. It's like those annoying game show hosts that say we will announce the decision after the ad break."

"Okay, I promise I will bring my journal with me tomorrow and share my experiences with you," Dan said.

"Okay. I'll see you then, and don't forget to bring your journal."

"I won't, Danny Boy. See you then."

***

THE FIRST RAYS OF light painted the morning sky in a beautiful pink and grey canvas. Dan called it a 'galah dawn' because it reminded him of his favourite pink and grey bird. The tide was out, the swell was up and much to Dan's relief, he was the only person on the beach. The early morning solitude wrapped him like a warm blanket, but the wind soon brought him back to reality as he adjusted his beany and gloves. As complicated as Dan liked to make life, the simplicity and beauty that surrounded him was a reminder that his needs were simple and they were being met. Dan was filled with gratitude and peace. He felt good. Breathing in the cool morning air, he gave thanks to his A Team and watched as Munay chased the incoming wash at full pace. As the wave reached the shore, she would turn chest on and let the wash splash over her. It was a game she had created and never failed to bring a smile to Dan's face.

Dan had dug out his journal the night before and had started recounting what he had written. The thing that struck him immediately was that it had been ten years since he had gone to Peru. The other thing that stood out was what Dan had learnt at the time but not actioned. Awareness without action was one of Dan's pet hates, yet as he read on, he understood that at the time he hadn't been fully ready, and it was only with subsequent learning that he was now ready to do his Pachamama homework. He had certainly put some things into action, but there was also an unfulfilled opportunity remaining. He was looking forward to sharing his adventures with Danny. Dan enjoyed Danny's youthful curiosity and cheekiness and had begun to really enjoy and look forward to their time together. In a way, spending time with Danny took away some of the sadness of not being able to share in his own kid's lives at the same age.

Time to switch your mind off and just feel everything around you, Dan.

Who said you had to die to live in heaven?

※※※

"HEY, DAN. I HOPE that's your journal under your arm," Danny called out.

"Good morning, Danny Boy. Decided to skip the pleasantries today, hey?"

"Oh sorry, I'm just excited to hear all about your experiences in Peru!"

"Yes mate, it is my journal. Would you prefer I read to you, or would you like to read it yourself?"

"I would like to hear your story from you."

"Get comfortable then. It will take a while."

"Ready when you are…"

3-5 June 2014

After struggling for over two weeks to find a holiday for my wife and I, and whilst still coming to terms with two redundancies in twelve months, I asked for guidance and to be open to the right opportunity. In asking, it was both personal and job related because I felt lost, unsure and not in a position to make any decisions. I had considered the South American healing previously, but never acted. Whilst riding my bike, it came to me very clearly that I had to go to South America *for me*, and from there, all else would flow.

Within two days and with the love and blessing of my wife, I was booked and committed to going. Things fell into place and whilst being taken aback by committing to something on a whim, I felt excited and ready to confront *me* and everything that was holding me back. Someone came to me in a dream and comforted me on the way forward and what was to come. I felt reassured and certain that the people I had chosen to guide me were the right people and that the experience had the potential to be truly life changing. I haven't done anything alone and just for myself for as long as I can remember.

My wife is my rock and the love of my life, who I will miss and possibly call for on this journey. She is my life and my strength, and I look forward to coming home to her as a better person. Being a better person is my journey, the benefits from which I can share.

8 June 2014

I fly out in just over two hours and have said my goodbyes. I found saying goodbye very hard because I love my wife so very much and am not used to not doing things together. I've felt scared since waking up this morning. I know that what I'm doing is important for me and is the right thing to do. But now that the time has come to commence this journey, I am realising the magnitude of what I'm doing. I go with an open heart and expect that this journey will be defining in my life.

I had a non-eventful flight to Dubai but only slept for one hour, so hopefully with relaxation music and a good seat, I will sleep on the fourteen-hour leg to Rio De Janeiro. I have calmed down now and am feeling relaxed.

Well, that good sleep failed to happen! The plane was chock-a-block full of people travelling to the Football World Cup in Brazil. Now I am just in the "travel zone", existing from nap to nap. Thankfully the flight to Buenos Ares wasn't packed and transiting through customs only took twenty minutes. I now have an eight-hour transit in the airport and am like a homeless vagrant walking the boards. I am certainly learning to be patient and accustomed to waiting.

I doubt I will ever forget how long eight hours at Buenos Ares airport can be. I was bored shitless, didn't sleep and walked the length of the airport over forty times. The flight to Lima was uneventful and the transit smooth. Amongst all my frustrations with a lack of sleep and travel time, I have taken the time to be grateful that I haven't had any issues with immigration or security at all.

My final leg to Cusco was short and bumpy. I was met by Marco, so after more than fifty hours, I arrived at Los Apus for a well-earned sleep.

10-11 June 2014

I am sleeping lots and am getting over my initial altitude headache. My sleep is still broken and often at the wrong time, but I feel I'm regaining "condition", post travel. Cusco has changed since I was last here. There is more badgering to buy trinkets and there are more beggars on the street. That said it still has a magical feeling. There was a flower festival with school kids in traditional dress dancing around the square. The colour, noise and joyous energies were amazing, as were the crowds who came to watch and cheer.

I heard news from a colleague in Australia that the company we had both worked for was ceasing its operations completely. It brought back lots of emotions and thoughts and galvanised in me the significance of this journey. I am at a significant crossroad in my life right now. I need time to heal and insight into the way forward. I know there will be different paths and choices. I just want to be positioned to be open to choosing the right ones. I understand that I am responsible for the choices I make and can't rely on anyone but myself to make things happen. I have demons to face, uncertainty to conquer and peace to find. Lying awake at 2:30am, it sounds and seems simple. But we will see what I think, write and say in six days' time. It all starts tomorrow with the Andean Volcanic Colonic. Be an open, honest and courageous grasshopper and all will be revealed. I need the tears to flow unrestrictedly and the sadness and hurt to be honoured and released. I need to truly find love and respect for who I am and find and honour my true purpose.

12 June 2014

Today I learnt that 'ayahuasca' is a Quechuan word that translates to 'vine of the soul'. Ayahuasca comprises of roots from the B.Caapi vine (the masculine) and the leaves of the Chacruna plant (the feminine). Both need to be in equal proportion to be effective and have no effect in isolation of each other. The masculine B.Caapi supports physical healing whilst the feminine Chacruna supports spiritual/emotional healing. I found this out at a shop run by the organisation I was doing the ceremonies with in Cusco, which I found in my wanderings. The shop was filled with mandalas depicting people's associations with their journey, which were colourful and amazing to see. Whilst in the shop, I was told that a couple from New Zealand and single guy from America would be joining me on my retreat. The whole experience at the shop was positive. I don't think I needed any reassurance, but I got it and am really looking forward to the retreat. I am blessed and soon to be unburdened. Thank you spirit for your blessings.

13 June 2014

Today was the purgative volcanic water cleanse. I was met at the hotel by a puffing and exhausted lady who had carried about ten litres of water plus medical examination equipment about 800m from her car. After letting her know that I had checked out of my hotel, she said she had hoped to do the cleansing in my room. With that not happening, she called a taxi, and we went on a "Cusco ride" around the city square, which was still closed as part of the ongoing flower festival. We went into some very basic parts of town and at the time all I could think of was what a leap of faith I had undertaken. I could've been kidnapped for all I knew, but we eventually arrived safely at a hostel where I was to complete the cleanse. The lady's name was Faith, who was a registered nurse. She had a lovely personality and big beaming smile which made me feel comfortable and relaxed. With my blood pressure high (158/89) and weighing 80kg, I started the process.

The volcanic water was high in minerals and salts. It didn't taste too bad, but it was designed to go through you like a dose of salts. I was required to drink 5 x 375ml glasses of water then walk up and down six flights of stairs five times, then back for another five glasses of water. I started to get full and after drinking the tenth glass, my gall bladder was overfilled, and I promptly threw it back up. From there, it was back to the stairs for ten more repetitions. Finally, I felt the need to go to the toilet. After going the first time I realised there was no toilet paper, and that the toilet wouldn't flush. I asked for paper, but English wasn't Faith's strength, so the purge was to occur without paper. What else are jocks for, right?

On the third purge and with a very full and smelly bowl, I found the water valve to the toilet and thankfully I was able to flush. Three more glasses of water and numerous more trips to the loo until all I passed was water and it was clear, saw me done. Faith complimented me on only needing ten glasses before the first trip, as apparently it can take some people up to twenty-five glasses. I was instructed to wait at the hostel for another hour because the need to go wouldn't stop immediately.

Faith disappeared, and whilst I was waiting for the hour to pass, I realised I didn't know where I was and how to get back to where I'd been staying. Somehow, I had mucked up the number of nights' accommodation I needed before the retreat and hoped they had a room available for the night. It also dawned on me I could have asked them when Faith arrived and saved myself from the adventure of finding my way back. I'll put it down to the effects of altitude lol.

I found my way back with the help of smiling locals and booked another night's accommodation. But at the end of the day, I felt very weak and tired. The whole purpose of the cleansing was to support the absorption and effectiveness of the medicine I was to take in the ceremonies. It was a very thorough process, but I think it was more the number of stairs at altitude that stuffed me. It all starts in earnest tomorrow. I will lose contact with the world for the next five days and the noble silence (no talking) starts the moment I am picked up at 9am. I am excited about what is to come but expect it will be tough both mentally and physically. I am up for it, after all that's why I am here.

14 June 2014

The retreat starts today. I was sitting in the stillness after I woke at about 3:30am. I felt my father's energy and that of The Father. I had tingles throughout my body, and I cried freely. I expect connection with both fathers could be significant in the next five days. That connection, bringing light into my heart and having clarity of my life's path and the way forward, are all the things I want to work on. I also want to remove self-doubt and forgive myself and understand a way back to my daughter. I seek joy in my heart and light in my soul. I have no fear, just hope and opportunity.

Like everything else, the trip to the retreat location was, through normal eyes, not normal. We drove through the city streets and then took a turn up a dirt road. It was washed away, and the car bottomed out. It felt like we were going to a certain "ransom" and then we were there. Rustic but functional. On the way here I shared the ride with the Kiwi couple who were travelling the world.

I'm sharing a room with an Indian American, but it's impossible to know what he's like because of the noble silence. We met our first shaman who is going to take us through a coca leaf reading and the purification and cleansing ceremonies. He is everything you expect a shaman to look like and is sincere and genuine. He has an honest energy and a big silver teeth smile. He is warm, caring and real. It will be a different shaman who conducts the ayahuasca ceremony who we are yet to meet. I feel like the floodgates are going to open and I will experience true healing and connection. I am open in honesty to get the most from the experience. Vishal is my roommate's name, and the Kiwi couple are Dianna and James. We are all on this journey together.

"I guess that sets the scene, Danny Boy. Any questions so far?"

"No thanks," Danny responded.

"You're unusually quiet. Are you okay, mate? I can't remember a time when you didn't have a question."

"Yes, Dan. I'm just intrigued by what you've shared."

"Why intrigued, mate?"

"You seem to have had the awareness of what needed to change and understood the opportunity that lay in front of you, yet you are only now putting it into action ten years later."

"Perceptive as ever, Danny Boy. That's what being ready truly means. I have known the opportunity for over ten years, but I have had to learn and understand so many other things to be able to join the dots and build my desire and need for change. In hindsight, this whole experience was the first step in putting awareness into action. My starting point was emotional healing, forgiveness, and spiritual connection. As part of the first day, a shaman did a coca leaf reading for me. It was incredibly accurate and included references to some things only I knew and hadn't shared with anyone. The shamans key feedback was that my spiritual health was poor and bordering on dead. He described it by saying the creator's light within me was very dull and barely flickering. He encouraged me to build my spiritual connection with the creator and warned me that If I didn't, I would likely physically die.

"He then went on to describe what he called my 'big

suffering': my relationship with my kids. He reiterated that it was important I never give up trying to build a relationship with them and that it was critical I maintain contact with them. He said they needed the influence of a father and that I needed to speak my truth and be open and honest with them. As I wrote in 'A Father's Promise' there were many times I felt like giving up, but I am so glad I didn't. If not for this experience and the love and support of my wife at the time, I easily could have. It was my big suffering. I loved my kids and wanted to be a part of their lives but at that point, they still felt lost to me; 'somewhere over the rainbow', out of reach. The shaman then went on to explain the state and health of other family members, then circled back to my spiritual health. He said I had a spiritual block. I had a connection but hadn't put anything into action. He encouraged me to put more effort into my spiritual health and trust more in myself and my heart/gut feeling. He said I was connected but needed to turn on the light inside and believe in myself so others could hear and understand my truth. He said it was time to let go and forgive because the flame from the candle was very dim. The shaman finished with some insights around work and said there were good prospects if I make my own company and worked for myself. He said it may take time so go with the flow and don't worry about it."

"Isn't that where you are now, Dan?" Danny asked. "I mean, working for yourself in your own company?"

"Yes, it is. But it's the second attempt. In between,

I formed a company with an ex-colleague and good friend that didn't work out. The experience led to me having an emotional breakdown. I am the type of person that becomes immovable once I commit to something. I thought I was committed and couldn't understand why I wasn't prepared to find a way to make the business successful. I have since realised that I had created and forced the idea, and that it came from my thinking, not universal flow.

"Without being called by Pachamama, I had gone back to Peru and did ayahuasca again. Nothing in that second experience flowed. I suffered severe altitude sickness, and I constantly felt like I was about to have a heart attack. I only did one ceremony and felt that if I did any more, I would die. I hadn't completed my homework from the first experience, and without knowing, I was looking for a quick fix and was deceiving myself. I had convinced myself that it was the right opportunity, but in hindsight I realised in my heart, it wasn't. It was another example of a personal pattern of behaviour where I created co-dependency because I didn't trust in my own ability. It still saddens me to remember the impact that my failing had on someone I truly respect, value and admire. Whilst we are still in contact, I placed an incredible strain on our friendship that likely will never be the same. I can't change what I did, but I can own it and learn from it, which is the only way I can honour a dear friend. He remains the most talented, gifted and kindest person I have had the privilege to work with and know.

"What the shaman had said about my spiritual

connection being there but not actioned upon really resonated with me. In terms of all things spiritual, I held the belief that unless the message was 'sledgehammer subtle' I wouldn't get it or understand it. Whilst not entirely true, it was my limiting belief. Prior to the first ceremony I remember asking for clear 'sledgehammer subtle' understanding from my experience. Pachamama heard me and all I can say is she has a great sense of humour."

"What happened? Did you write about it in your journal?"

"Yes, I did, Danny Boy..."

My First Ayahuasca Ceremony

Wow, what an amazing experience. I started slowly and after the first cup, I had no visions or insights. I was offered more medicine which I took but then threw up before the required fifteen minutes. This was a huge insult to Pachamama and her gift. So, as always, I tried to hide my shame away and felt very bad about myself. Whilst the others seemed to go in and out of trances, I doggedly resisted letting go. I wasn't prepared to get out of my head and into my heart. Instead, I lay there feeling guilty about my disrespectful act. As others finished their journey, and were ushered off to sleep, I joined them, thinking I had failed. I couldn't sleep and kept processing my feelings until I humbly came to the point of praying to Mother Earth for forgiveness. I then bundled up my guilt and self-loathing and blew it to the universe. Within minutes, the block was gone, and The Mother took me into an altered state. I had previously seen short images but no visions. Then a vision came to me. I saw that I was a snake with a vibrant aqua marine colour on my side. The colours were in thin bands, not bold and strong. I then rolled over and saw my roommate, Vishal. His profile was that of an Inca statue. I rubbed my eyes, but the vision remained unaltered.

Once forgiven by The Mother, I started to have other visions and felt the need to vomit. I was in the middle of a vision and very dizzy on my feet, but I needed the bucket in the ceremony room. On making it to the bucket, I vomited and stayed in a trance-like state. The assistant woke up on hearing me and moved close to help and support me when, *WHAM*, I was hit with a bolt of lightning (a bit like a defibrillator effect). Such was the force of the shock that I jolted in reflex alarm and kicked the vomit all over the floor and the assistant, Paola. I was not aware of what I had done until I came out of my trance state. So, what was the cause? In my vision, I heard a rustling sound coming toward me which was getting louder and louder as it approached. I then saw a snake moving at the speed of light coming directly to me where it then coiled up ready to strike. Within an instant, it opened its mouth and took me into a world of white infiniteness. The speed in which everything happened was what caused me to convulse with such shock. Whilst clearly scared and startled by what I saw, I never felt any fear. Thank you, Mother, I certainly can't say the message wasn't "sledgehammer subtle".

The first ceremony was about the physical. I let something very significant go and have since learnt to package up doubt, fear and self-loathing into little bundles, and having asked for forgiveness, blown them to the universe. For the first time, I could send prayers of thanks and forgiveness from the heart. My heart, which for so long had been dead, is awakening.

P.S. my blood pressure was 158/100 and having been told my heart was not healthy, I spent half the night worrying I might die. Instead, I kicked a different bucket. And whilst I still haven't slept, I feel energised. I look forward to talking with the shaman to understand what it all meant.

We have now had a simple breakfast and will have our debrief and one on one with the shaman for two hours and then rest until tonight's ceremony, which will be about the spiritual. We remain in noble silence but can communicate with each other via gestures. It's a bit like playing charades.

I just had a memory from last night. Initially, I felt the shaman healing a piece of my heart. It was like synchronising my chakras, subtle but felt. I was told it wasn't the shaman who had done the heart healing; it was The Mother.

As part of the debrief, I found out I was the only one to connect from the heart with The Mother. The snake is Mother Nature. She jump-started my heart and there was light in my heart in places that had been dead and dormant. In some senses, it feels like new life, the shedding of old skin. It's not strong yet, but it will grow. Given the accuracy of the coca reading, to know my heart is physically crook is a real worry. I need to really change things to improve my physical health. Unlike my brother, I haven't been told it can't be cured.

Today, I am feeling the best I have in days. Last night cleared a lot of negative energy. I look forward to tonight's ceremony knowing that more magic will occur. The fear of not knowing what's going to happen is gone. I am now open to The Mother and look forward to connecting again and journeying together. I have so much to learn and understand. I learnt that blue is the colour of wisdom, which is what I'm surrounded by. I have beauty within and look forward to seeing and feeling it tonight. My candle burns dimly, but I'm slowly adding oxygen with the love and support of The Mother.

My Second Ayahuasca ceremony

If I thought the first ceremony was amazing, the second one completely blew my mind. I rewrote my life with the support of The Mother. One by one we brought unresolved matters of the past to the light and dealt with them. The healing was incredible. We worked on my heart and brought light to it. It was serious, fun, difficult and rewarding all meshed together. I went to my kids and reassured them that I was coming for them, to give them the unique love, support and guidance only a father can. I was coming to remove the dark cloak and bring unconditional love and possibility into their lives. I told my mother that I loved her and forgave her and that I had connected to the eternal spirit and that she could now pass with that knowledge. I held her hand and reassured her she would not die alone. I'm not sure if she has passed; I will know soon enough. I felt The Mother gliding through my body, healing as she went and bringing back things from the past to be dealt with. Some were known and some weren't. The biggest healing was sexual. It was deep, very, very deep and kept coming back throughout the six hours of the ceremony. I can't remember exactly what the healing was. Either way, it is dealt with. The Mother and I played the game of trust, belief and control. Every time I felt the need to stand up in an attempt to avoid what was happening, I couldn't. Mother kept saying, "have no fear, you won't shit yourself – trust me." This game went on for over eight hours.

It's now nearly 9am the next morning and I still haven't gone. I guess The Mother was right. I tried to escape over ten times, but with love and care, The Mother stopped me. It was all about facing the truth. There was a message about a pub for sale that I needed to investigate. We dealt with alcohol dependency, and I was assured I had the power to control and overcome addiction. I connected with my first wife and sent her on her way, wishing her happiness. I hold no feelings for her, and it was hard for me to connect, but I realised I had to forgive her and offer her unconditional love. I am free of her; the past is the past. I connected with my sweetest angel and promised to love, nurture and support her with my unconditional love, and to share more of me and the beauty that entails. I had a chat with the real me. No falseness, just genuine me. It reaffirmed that the greatest gift you can give is unconditional love. In giving, you receive plentifully. I sang, cried and laughed. I welcomed joy back and had fun. My inner child, whilst shy, was welcomed home. All in all, I changed the DNA of my life and started the transformation from darkness and sadness to happiness and hope. I have a true north. It has always been there. My true north is the belief in myself and truly listening to my heart. I can do anything, as long as it comes from truth. I only have to believe in myself and trust. As the shaman subsequently said to me, "You are the best shaman and healer for you. You know yourself better than anyone and have the power to heal yourself."

The Mother shared the beauty of the snake with me. I now understand that dancing cobras are merely dancing in the glow of The Mother's love. I am a proud snake: loyal, loving, protective and giving. I am not evil nor dangerous. I am beautiful, strong and proud. I have light, I have connection. I am unconditional love. I don't have to lament that my daughter is somewhere over the rainbow, because I realised I can join her wherever, and we can fly together.

I have some more travelling to do. I need to go and see my children and my mother and tell them the truth from my heart. I need to see my brother and tell him I am prepared to love and guide his son should something happen. I need to spend time with my brother alone to love and support him and to help him open up.

I have been reborn!

I have a clear mind.

I have the above to do and so much more.

But I am alive!

I have passion and I have purpose.

Un-freaken-believable – how exciting, I am dying to live! Wow, I feel like this, and I still have one ceremony left. Goodness knows what's to come. Whatever it is, I am open to receiving the gift with love, gratitude and light in my heart.

I'm sitting beside a flowing creek. The sun is shining, and it is warm on my skin. I can only see, hear and feel nature all around me. If not for being here and answering this calling, I feel certain that I would have died. I haven't wasted the gift of love; more so, I haven't given it. It's now time to honour the love and unique gift in my heart that is me. To share it unconditionally – to give. That's where passion comes from, where joy and laughter live, where happiness has no limit. From there is where everything flows.

Connection is light, light is love, love is peace and peace is happiness.

Happiness is living with joy in the service of others.

It doesn't matter what I end up doing when I return, as long as it comes from the heart and supports the continuous flow of happiness. It will match a sense of purpose, and it will bring light, happiness and joy to others because it will flow and nourish me. It is so beautiful to be at one with Mother Nature. In nature is where love and beauty flow, not in a contained sterile benign place. My connection to nature is back. I need to spend more time in connection and in nature. How that connection is maximised is yet to be fully understood, but I feel I can live my dreams and live in a place of peace with nature and share the wonders of positive light and love. A place where people can heal and where I can flourish and feed my soul. I know what – I'm working on the how – and soon I will know the when.

My Third Ayahuasca Ceremony

I'm physically and emotionally spent! Again, I had some amazing learnings and experiences. I still have blocks, but when I look back on this journey, I can only marvel at how far I have come. Whereas a week ago, I would have been self-critical and turned things into negative energy, I now simply accept with humour that a brick is porous but sometimes it takes a while for things to sink in. I am at the start of my spiritual evolution and the progress in five days has been exceptional. The first key lesson of the third ceremony was to open your eyes. I was lying there, eyes closed, waiting to see visions. Nothing was happening and then The Mother, in good humour, gave me a "sledgehammer subtle" message to open my eyes. I did, and straight away I saw Aztec type designs in colours of chocolate, beige and cream. The designs then morphed into the scales of a snake and were an amazingly beautiful pattern. The shaman was chanting and then his chant changed to an Aboriginal sounding song, and I was connected to the outback by both land and Indigenous people. I saw myself as a champion of their cause, which surprised me. I then saw a white trident and a beautiful stag deer. The light was pure and the vision majestic. I see both as being God, The Creator letting me know they are always there to guide me. I got answers to questions about the next steps for work. They were not crystal clear so I will reflect on them when I have more energy. The shaman confirmed the trident and stag were in fact my father who had died when I was eighteen months old, showing me that he was with me and supporting and guiding me through my life. He further confirmed that the brilliantly vivid aqua marine colours I'd seen represented sea creatures and my connection to the ocean. Everything the shaman shared was insightful and powerful. His final comment was his greatest gift to me. He said, **"you are your greatest shaman and healer. You have the ability to heal yourself."**

"Wow, what an amazing experience, Dan. You are quite the storyteller."

"Thanks, mate. But that barely scratches the surface of the whole experience. My learnings behind the significance of the rituals and practices performed by the shaman made the ceremonies even more special. The shaman sang songs, called Icaros, to guide and support me on my journey. In my case, the shaman worked his butt off to help me relax and connect. At times I felt sorry for him, but he never wavered in his commitment to supporting my journey and healing. I can't adequately describe the healing I felt from The Mother as she glided through my body. It was the most amazing thing I have ever felt in my life. Rather than being about visions, my journey was more about healing. I had a lot of negative energy to clear. Part of the natural response to the medicine is to throw up. I remember looking into the bucket and seeing dark and evil faces staring back at me. I started to growl at them every time I threw up, to force the negativity out of me. I knew at the time I was growling at myself. I had so much to clear and purge, but it was all a part of preparing me for the healing process that followed. I was being honest when I wrote that I likely would have died had I not gone there in response to my spiritual calling. It was a life-changing experience I will never forget."

"There were some interesting things you mentioned about welcoming your inner child home and deep sexual healing," Danny said. "Have you made any more sense of that?"

"Not specifically, mate. There was so much I learnt and applied but so much else that got lost in the noise of life when I got home. As I shared, I have known some opportunities for a long time but I've not done the work. They say The Mother gives you homework to complete, lessons to learn, before you can be open to and see the next opportunity as part of your spiritual evolution. Ten years sounds like a long time, but I have been learning and growing the entire time. Whilst I haven't completed all my homework, I'm definitely getting closer with each passing day and year."

"Do you ever get tired and feel like giving up?"

"I sometimes get tired and frustrated, mate, but no, I never feel like giving up. I'm determined to reconnect with my true self in this lifetime and honour the lessons The Mother has taught me."

"So, what homework do you still have to do, Dan?"

"Mate, as Michael Jackson sang, I need to work on my relationship with 'the man in the mirror'."

Danny shook his head. "Who's Michael Jackson?"

"Google him. **Forgiveness of others starts with forgiveness of yourself.** Whilst I have done a lot of work on forgiving others, I haven't been able to fully let some things go. I have become less self-critical, but I have also created lifelong patterns of behaviour that take time to change. To truly give of yourself in the service of others, you first need to give to yourself. It sounds selfish, but in fact it is the opposite. It's selfless. I don't recall being self-sabotaging and having low self-esteem when I was younger, so I need to unpack what changed."

"You never left school then?"

"What do you mean, Danny Boy?"

"Well, you still have homework to complete."

"You cheeky shit," Dan laughed. "You never stop learning in life, Danny Boy. I think the day you stop learning is the day you die."

"You mentioned you have become less self-critical. What changed?"

"Enough, mate. It's time to enjoy our surrounds and chill and relax for a while."

"Well, at least you know my first question when I see you tomorrow."

※※※

"HAPPY TUESDAY, DANNY BOY."

Danny perked up from his seat. "Hey, Dan. Did you see the dolphins?"

"Yes, I did, mate. I never tire of watching them. They are so playful and majestic at the same time. I even saw a seal surfing the waves. Whenever I see a lone seal, I call it UV."

"UV? Like ultraviolet?"

"No, mate. It all links back to Covid."

"Covid?" Danny lifted a brow. "Your mind certainly works in funny ways."

"That it does, but it makes perfect sense if you know the story behind it. Yesterday you were asking what I had already done to become less self-critical. Outside of the amazing healing in Peru, I started to listen to my intuition more. My true self comes from connection and knows what is right and good for me, so instead of dismissing it, I started to trust my intuition.

"At the start of Covid, I was caretaking a caravan park. I had been in the area for just under twelve months and the only certainty I had was not going back to what life had been. Working in the caravan park had been humbling. At the start, I thought I had gone from the penthouse to cleaning the shithouse again, but then realised it was what

I needed to do. The experience helped me to stop feeding my ego, and for the first time, I felt gratitude. As simple as my role was, it was the first regular paid work I'd had in over two years. The job provided me with the means and time to accelerate my personal transformation and learning in a place I loved. I had brought myself to the point of emotional exhaustion and breakdown and was finally able to let go of control and trust the creator and my A Team. I always felt loved and supported, and whilst I was alone, it was where I needed to be to learn what I needed to learn. I thought I had already been brought to my knees, but then came the pandemic.

"Like most people, in the early stages I believed what I was told about the outbreak of a deadly disease, but in time, I started to question the validity of the measures taken and the narrative. I couldn't understand all the new restrictions and limitations that were put in place around a disease that had a high survival rate and was not dissimilar to a bad strain of the seasonal flu. I had been practicing natural health for over ten years and was fit, healthy and on no medications. I'd also developed a distrust for the pharmaceutical industry, which I saw as being more about profit and self-interest than wellness. At the time, I chose to not get vaccinated, and just wanted the freedom of choice as to what I put into my body. It wasn't about being right or wrong; it was all about freedom of choice. I accepted others who wanted to make a different choice to mine and only sought the same in return. Instead, I was labelled an 'antivaxxer' and berated for 'putting others at risk'. Freedom of choice was forcibly removed during the pandemic, and history will show that rather than being a diabolical pandemic, it was a 'scamdemic' that caused so much unnecessary emotional and physical pain and suffering. My heart still goes out to all those who consequently lost their loved ones, jobs, livelihood and health.

"In the early stages of the pandemic, I remember walking along the beach with Munay, when I noticed a small seal pup beside us in the wash. It was only tiny and looked very young. It began to follow us along the beach. It was swimming on its back less than ten meters away, and not alarmed in the slightest. I sensed it just wanted company and that it was scared and felt very alone and vulnerable. We saw it for the next four days, where it swam with us for the length of our walk and then it was gone. I had been under significant pressure from my family and employer to get vaccinated. In my heart, I knew it was the wrong thing for me. The pressure was amplified when my employer enacted a 'no jab, no job' policy. What made the situation worse was that I was in employer provided accommodation, which meant not only would I have no job, I also wouldn't have a roof over my head. It was coming into peak holiday season and the likelihood of finding pet friendly accommodation was very low. The easy decision was to park my gut feeling, beliefs and health values, and just get the jab. I finally relented under extreme pressure and duress and decided to get the jab.

"The decision went against my will and better judgement. Thankfully, however, when I told my employer I was prepared to get the jab, I was told it was too late and they'd already found a replacement for my job. I remain unvaccinated, grateful and thankful for the protection from my A Team. Whilst I was prepared to cave in at the time, I learnt that I would never make that same decision again. I learnt to stand in my truth."

"That's interesting. But what's it got to do with UV?" Danny asked.

"Subtle as ever, Danny Boy. After seeing the seal pup, I wrote a short story about what I was feeling. I felt vulnerable, alone and uncertain, just like the seal pup. I called the seal UV because their plight mirrored that of the unvaccinated (UV)."

UV The Seal

UV was born a free spirit and loved to swim and play in the sea. He frolicked in the waves and loved the warmth of the sun on his skin as he lazed on the beach. UV was surrounded by his family who he loved. He used to dream and imagine all kinds of things and felt happy and free.

When he was only a young pup, UV experienced the deepest sadness when his father failed to return from catching fish to feed his family. UV loved his dad and missed him every day, but knew he could call on his father at any time and feel his love because his father was always with him in his heart. It had been hard for UV's family to survive without their father, but they found a way by loving and caring for each other and contributing in any way they could. Their family bond forged from love was impenetrable.

As UV got older, he became unhappy with all the rules that he had to follow but he knew they were to help him stay safe and belong. From an early age, UV had become mischievous and rebellious and sought ways to stay happy and free. Eventually, though, he withdrew into himself, did as he was told, but lost the joy, happiness and freedom he had once felt inside. Many years later, UV decided to go on an adventure to rediscover what he had lost. That very adventure had brought him to this moment in time where he was alone, frightened and uncertain about what to do.

UV was swimming in the shallows close to the shore. He let out a wry smile as he contemplated the irony that his adventure to find happiness and freedom now left him feeling trapped. He was close to shore because he was being relentlessly hunted by a large pack of sharks. They stalked him from the deeper water ready to make a light snack of him. Whilst there were enough small fish to feed him for now, he knew he couldn't survive for too long this close to shore.

UV felt vulnerable and struggled with the consequences of the choice that had led him here. He was isolated from his family and friends and longed to see them all again. How he wished he could swim and play and share the love he had for them, and feel their love for him.

Startled from his thoughts, UV saw a man staring at him from the beach. Immediately diving for safety, when he resurfaced, he realised he knew the man. His name was Mr Astra, who beckoned UV to come up onto the beach. Mr Astra promised he would protect UV and make him safe. He had met Mr Astra many years before, and whilst he had appeared well intentioned, UV knew his motives and promises were hollow. When UV's best friend and then his sister had become sick, they had trusted Mr Astra's promise to make them well again. Instead, UV had watched them both die a long and painful death. That memory had left a deep sadness in his soul but an even stronger resolve to not fall prey to the same fate. In his lifetime, UV had already lost too many family and friends that he loved to Mr Astra's unfulfilled promises. Whilst he would no longer be trapped by the sharks, he knew in his heart that this was not his path to freedom.

UV again dived for cover and swam away underneath the water, fearing the temptation to change his mind. When he hit the surface, he heard a whisper on the waves as he had as a child. He could hear his father's voice saying, "freedom, happiness and joy all still live within you, son. You only feel trapped by your fear. Trust the truth in your heart and you will always find a way." With this knowing, UV mustered all his courage, cried, "freedom," and swam out to sea.

"That's so cool, Dan," Danny said, eyes wide with intrigue. "So, what did you do?"

"I was lucky to find a campsite in Kalaru, so whilst effectively homeless, I had a tent and of course, Munay. It was in that time of absolute uncertainty that I connected strongly with The Creator and my A Team, and just let go and went with the flow. It wasn't without stress or concern, but in the end, I gave up trying to make something happen and trusted that things would work out. I approached the local real estate agents, who all said they had nothing available. Five minutes after leaving the last agency, my phone rang, and it was the lady I had just been speaking with. She said that on reflection, there was a place in Yellow Pinch that hadn't been listed or advertised yet that might suit. It did, and I'm still there nearly three years later. It's a beautiful, peaceful and magical place that I am blessed to call home. It's surrounded by nature and feeds my soul every second I am there. It's been a tree change that has complemented my sea change and it fills me with gratitude. I have been so blessed to be led to such a 'Dan space'.

"When I was in Kalaru, I also met my first client. Each morning, I took Munay for a walk on Tathra Beach. One morning, I ran into a guy walking a young pup. We struck up a conversation. I spoke honestly and philosophically and shared that I was considering establishing a coaching and mentoring business. I was taken aback when he said he would like to be my first client and to call him once I got going. It wasn't a coincidence we met. He had established a business from scratch that now employed over a hundred people. What struck me about him was his openness to learn and his genuine care for others. We are more like friends now and are still working together. It's a friendship of mutual benefit. I have learnt so much from him in return and am forever grateful to him for seeing something in me that at the time I didn't trust.

"From connection and without coincidence, coaching and mentoring was affirmed as my purpose. I had been encouraged by others to coach and mentor based on their experience of me, but now I was ready, and saw it as a clear message of the direction I needed to take. I was then contacted out of the blue to do some work with a team in Central Queensland. Initially, the role was as a business improvement analyst, which isn't my strong point: data, analytics, charts and KPI dashboards are not what floats my boat. I was upfront and honest about that, and as much as I tried, I earned the nickname of 'Dashboard Dan' for all the promises made that the dashboard would be up and running next week, which sadly never happened. I was still able to build strong and positive relationships with the team members, which led to the opportunity of working in my sweet spot of leadership and personal development as a coach and mentor.

"It's been a special time full of ups and downs and plenty of personal learning. I am grateful for the opportunity and friendships gained. Working with the team can be like a game of snakes and ladders. Each day the dice is randomly thrown and we either land on a snake and go backwards, or hit a ladder and make progress. It's the same in life. We will all hit snakes and find ladders at different times and stages. The opportunity is to reduce the size of the snakes and increase the number of rungs in the ladders so when we inevitably hit a snake, we don't go all the way back to the start."

"What do you do with Munay when you're in Central Queensland?" Danny asked.

"I'm blessed to have two special ladies look after her for me. They treat her as their own and lavish her with lots of love and attention. They take her everywhere they go and treat her like the name they have given her: Princess. Without them, I wouldn't be able to do what I currently do. Munay loves them to bits, and whilst she misses me when I'm away, she readily adjusts to her princess lifestyle. Munay is my best mate, and we are constant companions when I am home."

"What do you need to do to be your own best mate, Dan?"

"As I said, Danny Boy, I'm working on it. Whilst you're googling Michael Jackson, search Robbie Williams as well, because like he says, 'Lord, I'm doing all I can, to be a better man.'"

"Haven't you already created a framework around how to unpack things?"

"What do you mean?" Dan asked.

"Let's synthesise everything you have shared with me, Dan."

"Thanks, Nik."

"Who's Nik?"

"He knows. Whatever! Let's join some dots..."

Externalise for satisfaction – internalise for opportunity.

- Release your anger and frustration. Focus on what's within your control to change and create awareness around what you could do differently to get a better outcome.

The power of what – ask what, not why.

- Use open ended "what" questions to stimulate new thinking, learning and opportunities. Remember, there is often no answer to asking "why" questions.

Know fear to have no fear.

- Understand and challenge your fears, self-talk, limiting beliefs and assumptions.

Think solution, not problem. What needs to change? Don't re-enforce the negative of failure (the problem).

You can't think your way to how you feel.

- What is your intuition or gut feeling telling you?

Change your association to change the outcome.

- Find the positive (opportunity), don't focus on the negative – "this is a gift of learning, not a punishment."

Accept that you are perfectly imperfect.
- Forgive yourself and your mistakes and focus on learning from them. Avoid comparing yourself to anyone else.

Awareness creates opportunity for change, not an excuse for not changing.
- What are you going to change or do differently?

Our reality is self-imposed.
- Change your current situation if you don't like it. That is true freedom of choice.

Believe you can and you will.
- "I can if…" "I can when…" I can change my life's story – it's my choice.

Seek help and support from your A Team or someone you trust.
- Know and trust you are safe and supported and never alone.

Never give in or stop trying. We are only the victims of our own choices and thinking.
- Change takes effort. You have the strength and ability to change any situation.

"I've never formalised it like that before," Dan said thoughtfully.

"It's fantastic that you have a process that helps support your learning."

"It is, Danny Boy. It doesn't have to be sequential either. You can apply any of the elements in any order that makes sense. The key is to apply the thinking to get the learning,"

Dan responded. "Thank you, Danny Boy. I love your challenges, your company and just hanging out and spending time together."

A single tear welled in Danny's eye and rolled down his cheek.

"What's wrong, mate?"

"I think you are finally ready, Dan."

"Ready for what?"

"To unpack your alcohol and self-love issues and understand what's been holding you back."

Dan's face dropped. "Danny Boy, you know I've been working on unpacking those issues."

"What's missing then? Are you looking for an answer or an excuse?"

"From tears to tyranny. Bloody hell, Danny Boy. You can be brutal."

"It's in our best interests that I am."

"*Our* best interest?" Dan frowned.

"Ced, you shared with me that you went from being an A Grade student and good boy, to being angry, resentful, rebellious and drinking heavily, using alcohol as a crutch. What changed or happened when you were my age? What caused you to lose your self-confidence and self-respect?"

"I don't want to talk about it."

"Running away again, hey Dan? Tucking it away, leaving it unresolved and just hoping things will change. Hope isn't a strategy, Dan. Trust in what you have learnt and everything you have shared with me."

"Piss off, mate!" Dan snapped. "What would you know anyway?"

"More than you think. It's time to practice your own preaching. Doesn't it start with externalising for satisfaction – internalising for opportunity?"

"Cheeky shit! Okay, I had gone from primary school to high school, but other than copping flack for being related to my brother and sister who were still at the school, I can't recall any issues."

"Think deeper, Dan. What changed?"

"I had a good set of friends, was good at sport and was popular and well liked."

"What else? What changed?"

"I was suffering growing pains. It was called something like Sever's Disease, where the bones in my heels were growing faster than the rest of my body. It was incredibly painful, and I was getting cortisone steroid injections."

"And?"

"My mum sent me to a sports medicine doctor who she had met through Little Athletics, to see if he could help me. He was working with one of the inner-city rugby league teams and had a practice in their league's club. Some shit happened but I dealt with it."

"What happened?" Danny pushed.

"It was something you don't forget, Danny Boy. But it's in the past and I would rather not talk about it. I can't change it anyway."

"Yes, you can. And you need to change the association

to change the outcome. What happened, Dan?"

"I went to see him, and he did an initial examination of my ankles and then suggested some machines that might help to reduce the pain. I used the machines as instructed and he then suggested that I come back each week for the next six weeks to get maximum benefit from the treatment. On the second visit, I had left straight from school and was still in my school uniform. It was winter so I had long pants on. When I arrived, he ushered me into his office, closed the door and said he needed to do another examination. Initially I thought nothing of it, even when he asked me to strip to my underwear and hop up onto the table. Whilst the problem was with my ankles, he explained to me that everything was connected in the human body, so he needed to feel and assess the tightness of all my muscles. Whilst feeling slightly uncomfortable with the way he went about the examination, once it was complete, I redressed and completed my treatment on the machines, like I had in the first week.

"The third visit started the same way as the second. I hadn't felt right about stripping down the week before, so I had gone in a tracksuit and was wearing shorts. He asked me to strip down to my underwear again. I hesitated but did as I was told. This time, after initially touching my lower legs, he removed my underwear, saying all my leg muscles were connected from my buttocks. I was lying face down when he began to fondle my bum and place his hands between my upper thighs. I felt very uncomfortable and didn't know what to do. My fear increased further when he asked me to roll over onto my back. I wasn't used to being naked in front of anyone and felt very exposed. He continued to fondle my body and then asked me to lie across his lap whilst he sat in a chair so he could check the elasticity of my muscles. I wanted to get up and run but I was frozen with fear. I did what I was told, and he continued to touch my bum and stroke my inner thighs. After about twenty minutes, he instructed me to get dressed and complete my treatment program. I got up and dressed quickly and ran away as fast as I could. I went home and told my mother what had happened and that I didn't want to go back. She said, 'he is a pillar of society and wouldn't do anything inappropriate to you.' She said he was just doing a full medical examination.

"Being taught to trust and respect authority, I went back for a fourth visit which was even worse. On arriving, I was ushered into his office where I saw there was another man. The doctor said the other man was another specialist and instructed me to strip down and hop up on the table. Again, he went to remove my underwear, but this time he started rubbing the front of my thighs and placed his hands on my penis. The stranger came to the table and started to touch me as well. I couldn't move and I went to yell out but couldn't make a sound. I was petrified with fear. I was then instructed to get up and lie across the stranger's lap in the chair for 'further examination'. It was at this point that the office door flew open and his secretary stormed in. The doctor became very angry and yelled at her to get out of his office. She stood her ground and pointed to me and said, 'I am not leaving until he comes with me.' What I experienced was bad enough, but I can only imagine what she saved me from that day. I thanked her and again ran as fast as I could to get away. This time I knew I would never go back. The lady probably lost her job for what she did, but I am so grateful and thankful to her for her courage that protected me that day. She saved me and I am forever indebted to her."

Tears welled in Dan's eyes as he looked at Danny Boy, who was sobbing. Emotions, long suppressed, flooded back into Dan's body as he too began to cry uncontrollably. They both cried until the horror was released for them both and they could cry no more.

"What did you do next?" Danny asked, still sniffing.

"I didn't know what to do, so I tucked it away and just found a way to move forward."

"At what cost?"

"What do you mean?"

"Can't you see that you have never dealt with what happened? And that you have been unnecessarily paying a price ever since. The patterns and habits you developed were all coping mechanisms. Join the dots, Dan. Your anger, rebellion, shame and abuse of alcohol all started after this happened."

"How do you deal with something like that? I haven't shared everything that happened," Dan said.

"I know."

"I was twelve years old, I was naïve, innocent and trusting and wasn't equipped to understand what happened, let alone deal with it. I kept asking myself why I didn't stop him. Why did I let it happen? Why didn't I get up and run away? Why did I go back? Why didn't my mother believe me and protect me?"

"It's time to ask what, not why..." Tears filled in Danny Boy's eyes. "This has cost us both so much over such a long period of time."

"You keep saying 'us'. What do you mean by that?" Dan asked.

"You left me in his office that day, Dan."

Dan's entire body stiffened. "What?"

"I'm your inner child, Dan. I am you. I was there with you and know everything that happened. I'm your source of joy, happiness, playfulness and dreams. You are the best mate I talked about who shut me out. As much as I tried, I couldn't reach you to help you. I was the innocence you left in his office that day. There have been times since where you briefly let me back in. Like in Peru. I cried freely that night. I was with you when you felt me for the first time in a long time. I have never left your side, or ever given up hope. I have longed for the day when you stopped running away and welcomed me back. I'm what's been missing in your life, Dan...

I am the cheeky and playful that offsets your seriousness,
I am the joyous that offsets your anger,
I am the happy that balances your sadness,
I am the fulfilment that offsets your emptiness,
I am the contentment that balances your dissatisfaction,
I am the self-love that balances your self-criticism."

Dan released a deep primal scream as he was racked with tears. "Oh, Danny Boy. I am so sorry! I didn't know what to do. I hated myself for letting him touch me. I hated myself for not stopping him. I hated myself for being a victim. I became angry and resentful of authority because it failed me. In the end, I couldn't cope with my shame. That's when I started to escape, to numb my pain. It was the only coping mechanism I could find. I have failed us both, Danny Boy."

"No, Dan, you haven't failed. You have finally accepted the need and created the opportunity to heal and truly move forward. We have allowed that man to impact our lives for too long. It's time to reclaim our freedom. We have learnt everything we need to help us move forward. I am so proud of you, Dan."

"Welcome home, Danny Boy. I love you."

"I love you too, Dan."

"That's been heavy."

"It must be time for a beer, Dan."

"Cheeky shit!" Dan chuckled. "We've got some work to do, mate."

"We do. Let's have some fun, Dan."

"It's time to break anchor, Danny Boy and sail at full speed into infinite possibility."

"You're a dreamer, Dan."

"No, smartarse. *We're* dreamers."

Acknowledgements

I would like to acknowledge and thank everyone that has been a part of my learning in this lifetime, especially those referenced in this story. You have all been my teachers and had a significant impact on my life. To my "A Team", your love, guidance, support and endless patience help me front up every day ready to learn and grow and be the best version of my true self. In you, I have connection and something to truly believe in. To my family, thank you for being there for the best and the worst of times. Iain, I can't thank you enough for capturing the essence of the story so accurately and illustrating it so beautifully. From the moment I reached out and you took my hand as a baby, we have had an unbreakable bond and connection that I will cherish forever. To all my beautiful children, thank you for accepting and never giving up on me. You all mean the world to me. Suzanna, thank you for all your efforts and first cut editing support in transforming my "blat" into English. Stephen, thank you for your encouragement and support and for stretching my thinking and belief in myself. Simple acts of kindness have far reached and often unseen impacts. To the OCC team in Tieri, thank you for your friendship and banter and for sharing the writing journey with me. You have helped me confirm my purpose and develop my coaching abilities through the good, the bad and the downright ugly. Carmen and Jill, thank you for making it possible for me to travel for work by looking after Munay. The love, devotion and care you show for her brings me so much comfort. I am truly grateful. Thank you to Sarah, Kaitlan, Gabby and the wonderful team at Greenhill Publishing for helping me Bring Danny Boy to life. And finally, I would like to thank Danny Boy. You are a special part of me that I cherish and won't lose contact with ever again.

About The Author

Dan lives on the far south coast of NSW near the seaside town of Merimbula. He has a strong affinity and connection with the sea and the bush which makes it the perfect place for him to recharge, dream and create. Dan is naturally curious and always seeking to learn and grow. He defines his purpose as, "sharing what I have learnt and learning what I haven't" which is why he is such a sort after and successful personal development coach and mentor. He is passionate about supporting others to make positive changes in their lives. Dan is also passionate about giving and will be donating 20% of all sales from this book and any associated new work to his two favorite charities, The Orangutan Project (TOP) www.orangutan.org.au and the Maguar Foundation (NFP) coming in 2025. Dan chooses not to have a social media profile. If you are interested in working with Dan, would like to engage him as a keynote speaker, or would like to provide him any feedback, please contact him at dan@spidan.com.au or check out his website at www.spidan.com.au

To order additional copies of this book please go to www.spidan.com.au

www.ingramcontent.com/pod-product-compliance
Lightning Source LLC
LaVergne TN
LVHW040155080526
838202LV00042B/3165